Tangled Threads Of Emotions

Subita Rooprai

BookLeaf Publishing

India | USA | UK

Dedication

To my mother, who has been patiently waiting for my first book and to the voice in my head that never gives me any wrong advice.

Preface

Dear Reader

I hope my poems brings you warmth and peace amidst the chaos of life. And that someone, somewhere would relate to them and it would bring a smile on their face.

May these poems be your companions on this journey, offering solace in moments of darkness and celebrating the bright spots of joy and reminding you of the intricate and beautiful emotions our heart feels.

I have written them with the ever lasting faith that ultimately everything falls in their rightful place, like my book is at this moment - In your hands!

Acknowledgements

I am thankful to my children, T&T (Tia & Tiger) and my husband for cheering me endlessly to publish my work.

A big thanks to BookLeaf Publishing for providing me with such an opportunity.

1. The Strength It Takes

It takes lots of strength to choose the right
It takes lots of will to stay in your lane,
The allure are quiet strong at time,
But it takes lots of discipline
To not give them a dime!

You say I'm lucky to have this life,
No one knows what strength it takes,
To walk on a path that's rightful,
You say luck favours me all the while,
No one counts the temptations that pile!

When its always your strength that governs
You know what kind of reputation you earn,
The wonderment that people think you hath,
No one knows what all you gave,
In order to walk on the righteous path!

I believe, destiny favours the brave,
Temptations bring despair that is grave,

Everyone keeps wondering what they did wrong,
No one wants to sing the confession song.
Life is full of rules and what you make of it,
All is on you - get disciplined or break it!

2. Unapologetically Old School

I'm quiet old school..
I walk by his side,
I provide suggestions subtly,
I don't enforce my presence anywhere,
Because the one watching from above
brings me centre stage as and when required..

I'm quiet old school..
I make my point,
I'm independent at things I do,
I make my own decisions too
But I'm not ashamed to walk behind him at times...

I'm quiet old school,
I believe in education,
I believe in evolving with time,
But I'm not the cool-dude nurturer,
who gives freedom today to weep tomorrow

I'm quiet old school..
I believe in fixing a problem,
I get thoughtfully angry too,
I don't trust others easily,
but I know where to hold on even with the eyes closed..

I'm quiet old school...
And quiet proud at that
I know by heart that sacrifices are to be made,
And to succeed, a decent price has to be paid..

3. Relations

Relations are difficult,
They don't come with their manual,
It all zeros down to the choices,
You either make them committed or casual

But the amazing thing about choices is,
They are never wrong when they are made,
It is only when the time passes by,
They are marked with their due grade.

Navigating relations is the toughest of all,
The joy, the sadness, the highs and the fall,
The chaos and excitement that travel along,
Brings you life that you so proudly belong.

4. Perception

Some would always consider you capable,
Some will underestimate you for your kindness,
Some will think how to benefit from you,
Whatever you do or say, you will find ways anew.
The world is a canvas thats vast and wide,
Move forward, keep painting it side by side,

Be kind, be true to yourself,
Don't take to heart what others perceive,
Its never too late to stand your ground,
Its never too late to create boundaries,
One heart might see you as a gentle touch,
Another might feel- Oh! you're too much.

You may have started behind the starting line,
Stories shall be whispered, both your and mine,
How you reached here, how much you bear,
No one really knows and no one does care,
The word we speak with careful art,
That mends one's soul can tear the other apart.

My words may bring you comfort, that is true,
Or make your sky gray instead of blue.

5. Gratitude

Oh, its a beautiful world,
Its the world I love to be in,
Its the world I always dreamt of,
With its fill of contentment and woes,
I won't still want to trade off the chaos.

With my soul filled with love,
For the emotions that I am around,
Whether its the joy of fulfilment,
Or the share of heartaches,
I would want it all for my sanity sake.

I own it all,
The elation and the fall,
They are mine to call,
I'm indebted to God for all that he gave,
My heart is always filled with gratitude,
I won't dream of any substitute

6. New Beginnings, New People

The family I married into, a different name,
A different history, altogether a different game.
I began with a hesitant step, a cautious glance,
A new set of rules like a brand new dance.
Their ways were unknown, their stories untold,
A generation woven, in the shades of old.

I entered the picture, a thread so new,
Trying to blend and yet be true.
There were moments of warmth and smile,
And moments of silence that stretched a mile.
I learnt their ways and the unspoken cues,
Navigated the traditions both old and new.

At times there was challenge, a difference in view,
A learning experience that was due.
I had built a bridge with patience and grace,
Found my footing in that new place.
With the passing of seasons and years,

My hesitant steps have conquered the fears.

A bond has been built, sturdy and strong,
Where love and acceptance rightfully belong.
They are my family now in every sense,
Through laughter, tears and debate intense
There are moments of joy and moments of strife,
We share a connection that enriches our life.

7. Little Joys of Life

A quiet moment, just to breathe,
To let the anxious thoughts release.
A cup of tea and a cozy chair,
A moment's peace beyond compare.
These tiny gifts, you give yourself,
Are worth more than a world of wealth.
They mend the spirit thats bruised and worn,
And greet the light of a new dawn.

Be kind to yourself and see,
The power in simplicity.
These small things softly understood,
Are signs of strength and doing good.

The sun dips low with air bound with dew
Painting the sky in shades of blue.
No rush, no race or a frantic pace,
Just quiet moments, time and space.
A steaming cup with a book in hand,
Entering the imaginary world across the land.

A simple meal shared with my kids,
Laughter and stories without any bids.
A cozy feeling thats quiet deep,
While these thoughts give me a peaceful sleep.
The warmth of sun on my kids' face,
Seeing my daughter talk with gentle grace.
These gifts of peace are so freely given,
A life relaxed and any remorse forgiven.

8. Breaking What Broke Us

The chains were forged in fire long ago,
A legacy of wounds, a silent woe.
Passed down like heirlooms, heavy and unseen,
Echoes of hurt in a bitter scene.
A heavy burden carried on each back,
A twisted path where love seemed to lack.

A mother's tears or a father's hardened stare,
The air filled with whispers of despair
I felt the weight of years I didn't know,
A seed of sorrow planted long ago.
But in the darkness an ember glowed,
A flicker of hope that bravely showed.

A yearning for a different kind of way,
To break the cycle and greet a brighter day.
I learned to listen to the voice in my head,
To make a choice and not just move ahead.
To heal the wounds that time had left unmasked,
To shed the past and the questions I never asked.

It was not easy, the path was steep and long,
But with each step, I grew brave and strong.
I learned to love, to forgive, to understand,
To break the chains at my own command.
And as I stand here, on this strong ground,
I see the seeds of healing all around.

9. Rainbow of Emotions

The rainbow arch is vibrant and bright,
A spectrum of emotions, day and night.
Violet is the mystery, deep and grand,
As if a sense of wonder is close at hand.
Indigo is wisdom of the soul,
Our intuitive mind making us whole.
Blue is the depths of ocean thats spread vast,
Sadness lingers where the shadows are cast.
Green is the calm of nature's grace,
With peaceful moments and a tranquil space.
Yellow is the sunshine so warm and clear,
Where happiness blossoms, banishing all the fear.
Orange is the zest of laughter's sound,
As if a playful jovial spirit is leaping around.
Red is the fire of a passion flame,
Burning with love and whispering a name.
The rainbow is a promise that shines above,
A spectrum of feelings and emotions, held in love.

10. Forgiveness

When the heart is in a clenched,
Stubborn fist holding tight to the hurt,
The grudge becomes a hungry thing,
Clawing at the heart that will not swing
Remembering hurtful words, a sharpened dart,
Embedded deep within the wounded heart.

Forgiveness doesn't come easy, my friend,
If you don't know the story and how it has end,
Its a word each one of us uses so light and free,
Its a fragile bird that doesn't easily flee
The cage of pain, the bars of spite,
The heart wants to avenge and balance it all right.

Forgiveness isn't forgoing all done wrong,
It is breaking free to where we actually belong.
It is not excusing what was done by someone,
But choosing light, thinking whats done is done.
Its an understanding,
That depends purely on the timing

Forgiveness is a gentle rain,
That washes sorrow, cleaning the window pane.
It clears the fog and the misty haze,
And lets us see life ahead in brighter ways.
It is a process, not an easy switch,
A slow untangling of threads, stitch by stitch.

So come and breathe in the air so sweet,
Forgiveness is a gift that is bittersweet.
Letting go of the pain is quiet a grace,
A healing balm for time and space.

11. Unspoken Goodbyes

Relations shift like the wind,
Soft and sudden, unpredictable
One moment, we are close,
Sinking into each other's rhythm,
Sharing secrets like they were always ours
Then out of nowhere a silence grows
Not loud, but heavy,
Like a cloud that drifts between us,
Casting shadows on the laughter
That used to fill the gaps
Things change,
Conversations feel different,
No longer effortless.
Our paths pull us
In separate directions,
Unseen forces at play.
Yet, I still carry pieces of you in my heart
The way we smiled when the world felt too much,
The moments we shared when time stood still,

The small gestures that were never spoken,
But understood.

12. Own Your Success

Its not important how you start in life,
Some start early, some get delayed,
Some start way behind the starting mark,
Some without brightness ahead, all in the dark

Where you are in life today..
Where you finally end up..
Where your perseverance gets you..
Is what matters at the end of the day.

Once you make your mark,
It no longer matters where you began,
No one will ask about the struggles you faced,
No one will see the uneven paths you raced.

What always matter is,
The place you stand tall today,
People will call it luck and fluke,
At such times, don't bother to retaliate
Just remember to give a smile and juke.

13. Happiness

Happiness differs for one and all
It could be anything around us
It could be the gentle breeze in a sunny day
Or your child's laughter,
seeing you when you enter your bay.
Its all within us, big or small,
Happiness is the thrill of the free fall.

It could be the fleeting moment
when you feel light and free,
Amidst the chaos of life,
when you find the calm.
It could be the warmth of love,
the words, the song,
That makes you believe,
it would be better soon,
and there will be a new dawn

Happiness is a strong shoulder,
you could rely on,

It could be the person,
to whom you belong.
Its the state of mind,
that is said to be strong,
Its the divine message sent,
saying nothing will ever go wrong.

14. The Warmth of My Mother's Yarn

With strands of wool and a gentle smile on her face,
She weaves yarn in beautiful colors that furls like lace,
Under the warmth of the winter sun,
My mother shares stories of the yarn weave that run.
Her laughter travels all over the place,
Each of her friends watch her animated face.

Everyone listens, adding their thoughts now and then,
She advices and listens to all like a mother hen.
Amidst this flow of conversation her needles click,
Making gentle sound and the design in her mind tick.

As the needles in her fingers come and go.
The yarn, a thread of vibrant hue,
a beautiful knitwear comes through.
Each stitch of wool is a memory spun,
A labor of love that carefully begun.

The knitwear continues to grow in her hand,

She crafts colorful patterns that look grand,
With a smile, she occasionally admires her work,
The delight of her friends a constant perk.

The hours melt, the sun starts to descend,
As her creation slowly transcend.
A sweater takes shape as a cozy wrap,
She then takes rest with a power nap.

The sweater grows with love instilled,
A gift of warmth so gently willed.
With each knit my mom says a silent prayer,
For her children, who this garment will wear.

15. A Faith So Strong

A whispered prayer in a silent plea,
A longing heart with dreams for eyes to see.
Beyond the veil, where shadows lie,
A hope unseen that will never die.
When doubts creep and darkness fall,
Faith answers with an immediate call.
Call me fatally optimistic with a trust within,
That hope will bloom and light will always win.

Not always clear is the path we tread,
But faith's soft voice dispels all dread.
A guiding star, divine's steady hand,
Will forever lead us across the land.
A promise kept with love so true,
A strength to see us safely through.
So let us grow this inner fire,
This unwavering, deep desire.
To trust and hope and to completely believe,
In the power of faith, we can all receive.

16. The Sibling Bond

A tangled mess of shared moments
Of whispered secrets about everything,
Of squabbles and playful fights,
And making up in moments of delight.
A bond unbreakable and deep,
A promise that we three vow to keep.

Through childhood dreams and teenage woes,
A constant love that continuously flows.
They know my quirks, my hidden fears,
They have wiped away my falling tears.
They've seen me at my worst,
And loved me still, with boundless thirst.
A shared history, hand in hand,
A bond that has a strong stand.

My brother is a gift, a hand to hold,
The ups and downs of life, a bond of gold.
All my sorrows, all my woes,
Its a wonder, how without words he knows,

He teases alot and sometimes fight,
But he is there for me, be it day or night.
A strength that never lets you fall,
He had never once ignored my phone call.
He understands my quirky and moody ways,
And celebrates all my brighter days.

My sister is a gift from the heavens above,
A bond of affection, a sea of love.
From childhood joys and burdens that we share,
To present responsibilities that we bear.
Through shared laughter and tears,
Together while raising my little munchkins,
My sister's support has been a comfort within.
She always borrowed my stuff and drove me insane,
But her presence in my world has been like a rainbow
after rain.

Our sibling bond is a precious thing,
A song my grateful heart will forever sing.
A special place and a sacred tie,
That will last in my heart, until the day I die.

17. Old Friends

A steady hand to hold,
a shoulder to lean, a listening ear,
a heart despite the distance which is quiet near.
with the laughter bright and shadows deep,
this bond that friendship vows to keep.

No judgments cast, no hidden sneer,
just understanding each other better,
with every passing year.
memories of our shared adventures side by side,
riding through life's unpredictable tide.

When skies are gray and our spirits low,
we find each other and plan a get together,
where we find old times and a knowing smile,
that makes the journey worthwhile.
lets raise a toast to friendships true,
a gift that sees us safely through.

18. My Treasure, So Precious

My dear children, you are my moonlit nights,
You both fill my world with shining lights.
From your non stop banter to curious eyes,
My heart fills with love so deep, it never dies.
You paint my days with laughter bright,
And chase away the darkest night.
With every stumble and every fall,
You both rise again, so brave and tall.

For me, you are gifts of sun and rain,
A symphony of both joy and pain.
I watch you grow, I watch you learn,
And with you, I too grow at every turn.
You question relations and emotions you see,
Exploring life which seems wild and free.
You both show boundless energy and grace,
A smile that lights up every place.

Through the wins, big and small, lessons are learned,

The knowledge of life is truthfully earned.
Its time to spread your wings and fly,
My love for you both will never die.
My precious children, you are my all,
I'll stand strong to catch you if you ever fall.
As a constant presence, strong and deep,
This is the promise that I'll always keep.

19. A Quiet Comfort

My anchor strong and in my stride,
Thats my life partner walking by my side.
Through choppy seas he is the one,
Whose love shines brighter than the sun.
No PDA major but a soothing balm,
His presence is comforting and calm.
A listening ear, a shoulder strong,
What I dreamt and now I belong.

No grand gestures just simple things,
The quiet comfort that he brings.
A steady shoulder that carries all,
He takes care of burdens big or small.
Man of a few words with a loving heart,
He worries for his family, the perfect part.
I have known him for decades few,
Still he manages to show a side so new.

We have weathered storms and also shared the sun,
Our journey, it seems has just begun.

With every passing year,
Our bond grows stronger and dear.
Raising the kids and finding their future,
Together we have guided each other like a teacher.
With every challenge hand in hand,
Together we had and will always stand.

His teasing jokes on me, with a silly grin,
My heart he always seems to win.
He sees the best in all I dream and do,
He pushes me to see them through.
I had always been practical and a planner,
But he came in my life in an unplanned manner,
For all he is and all he does,
The kids and I are grandly blessed

20. The Grief

A heavy heart, a world turned gray,
Where laughter fades and shadows play.
A vacant space, a silent room,
Where memories linger, wrapped in gloom.
A tear that falls, a whispered name,
A flickering candle, a dying flame.
The world moves on but time stands still,
Aching emptiness, a bitter pill.
The joy we knew, now lost and gone,
A fragile thread too quickly torn.
A hollow echo in the air,
A burden of grief, too hard to bear.
But even in the deepest night,
A tiny spark, a glimmer of light.
A seed of hope, though buried deep,
A promise whispered, secrets to keep.
For sorrow's touch, though sharp and keen,
Can mend the heart, and make it gleam.
And loss though painful leaves behind,
A love that's etched upon the mind.

So let the tears flow, let the heart grieve,
For in the mourning, we believe.
That love remains, though life may cease,
And sorrow's pain, will find its peace.

21. Small Wins

A single thread, so fine and frail,
Can snap beneath the slightest gale.
But woven with a hundred more,
A fabric made strong, it will endure.
These wins so small and meek,
A single word or a thought you speak,
A task completed maybe big or small,
They build a strength that conquers all.

Each little victory is a countable thread,
Through doubt and fear they grow
And as they gather day by day,
They chase the snippets of doubts away.
In all the efforts strong and true,
A greater self emerges through.
And what seemed daunting and vast,
Is conquered now and is meant to last.

A grain of sand thats alone and slight,
Can't move a mountain with all its might.

But billions joined make a shifting tide,
Can carve a canyon, deep and wide.
So let your small wins gather near,
Dispel the doubt and calm the fear.
Each tiny step and effort made,
Is a solid foundation thats gently laid.